This book is dedicated to the two most important people in the entire world to me. My sons, Khayree and Shane. This book is just one of many pieces of our legacy that we will build together. These pieces will live on way beyond all of our existence. I pray that you both reach the highest levels and succeed way beyond your own expectations.

Love,
Mom.

Printed in the United States of America
First Printing, 2020
ISBN 978-1-7923-4434-3

SUPER SHANE'S ALPHABET ADVENTURE

Written by
**Vanessa LaShawn Hall
and Shane Nixon**

Illustrated by
Whimsical Designs by CJ

Super Shane is super smart with superpowers right from the start. He can fly his way up high through the Alphabet stopping by each letter tower. Duck the showers, soak up the sun this will be fun for everyone!

So, come and fly with me learning letters A through Z. Would you like to come and learn with me?

Super Shane swooped his way to TOWER A where there are lots of Apples to eat while we play.

Next stop, on to
TOWER B

where Basketballs
bounce like
1,2,3.

TOWER C is for
Cars in three's
they drive so fast

OH WOW
OH WE!

Now we're on to TOWER D with Dinosaurs bigger than me.

Now, TOWER E
is the place to be
where Elephants fly
like birds and bees.

TOWER F
lives Flowers so Fresh
they smell so good;
I wish I could...

Get to TOWER G
where the Games are
free to play all day.

Let's Go I'll say.

TOWER H is where
the Horses race
to the finish line
just in time for...

TOWER I,
they eat Ice Cream pie,
it tasted so good,
I wish I could...

Come to TOWER J where
there is juice for days.
We can drink it all
and grow really tall.

On to TOWER K
where we fly Kites
and ride our bikes.

TOWER L
has lots of Ladders
to climb atop
and pitch to batters.

TOWER M
has Mounds of Mud
to kick around
all over town.

TOWER N
has Nacho bins
all filled with cheese.
May I have some please?

TOWER O is filled with
Oil to slip and slide
**Oh Boy,
Oh Boy,
Oh!**

TOWER P
has Pans of Pizza
filled with Pepperoni
for all the People.

TOWER Q
is for Quiet teens
who knit all day
making Quilts for Queens.

TOWER R
is for Racing cars
going really fast!
Who will win
who comes last?

TOWER S
is where Sharks
swim the best.

TOWER T
is Tall as can be
where Tigers play
on every Tuesday.

TOWER U
is Under the zoo,
its dark and scary
and Oh so hairy.

TOWER W
has Whales and bubbles
floating through the air
I wish you'd dare.

Come to TOWER X,
it's extra special,
playing Xylophones
while I sing my songs.

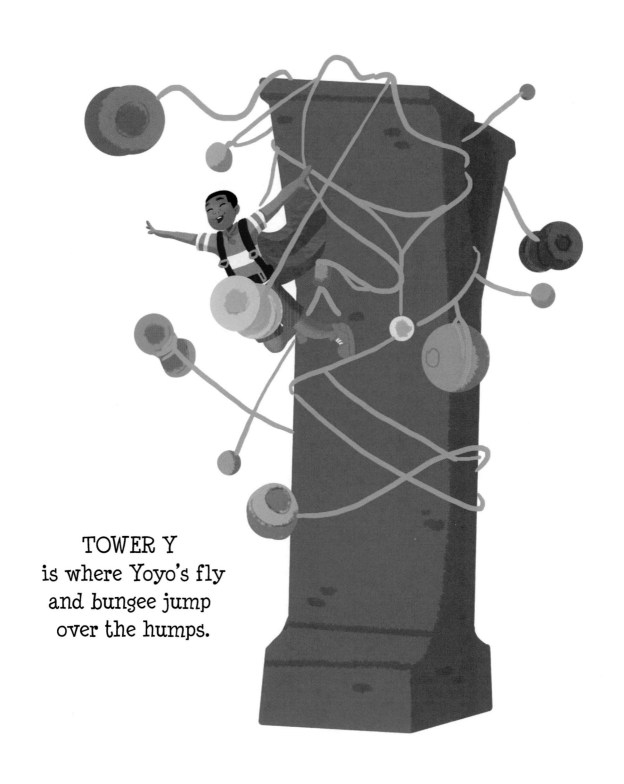

TOWER Y
is where Yoyo's fly
and bungee jump
over the humps.

Now, Tower Z has Zoo's of Zebras with many stripes to count I'll beat ya!

Now, back to Tower A, I can play all day! That was so much fun for everyone! Let us do it again with all of our friends from A to Z thanks for learning with me!

THE END

Made in the USA
Middletown, DE
27 September 2020